A LEFT-HANDER IN SOCIETY

Memoirs, Observations, Challenges, Research, Discoveries, and Imaginations of Patrice who is one of them

I believe some of this could also pertain to Right Handers - - because we are all in this life together. Following is some of my weathered wisdom - - and I am sure not everyone will agree!

Patrice Mosette

This book is a work of non-fiction. Unless otherwise noted, the author and the publisher make no explicit guarantees as to the accuracy of the information contained in this book and in some cases, names of people and places have been altered to protect their privacy.

WestBow Press books may be ordered through booksellers or by contacting:

WestBow Press
A Division of Thomas Nelson & Zondervan
1663 Liberty Drive
Bloomington, IN 47403
www.westbowpress.com
1 (866) 928-1240

ISBN: 978-1-9736-6363-8 (sc)
ISBN: 978-1-9736-6362-1 (e)

Library of Congress Control Number: 2019906451

Print information available on the last page.

WestBow Press rev. date: 4/17/2020

Is writing with the left hand an indicator of right brain dominance? Does left-handedness have a connection to dyslexia, or higher rate of dyslexia or exhibited ambidextrous versatility? This seems to be the logical related question to answer or share.

Could there be more involved in kinestheology communication with "energy " interworking?

Could DNA designate Right Brain and Left Brain and relate to ...

'...fearfully and wonderfully made... knitted in the womb...' ? Psalm 139:13

Are you a self-righteous "saint" who could "cut some slack" or not hold to a "higher standard" someone who is different from the perceived "right" thinking or actions?

This book is a MUST READ for encouragement, enlightenment, and entertainment.

CONTENTS

PART FIVE
ADDENDUM NOTES, AND RESEARCH AND SOURCE INFORMATION

INTRODUCTION

As a petite six-year old student, sitting at the little wooden desk in the first-grade classroom, I picked up my pencil and began to emulate the teacher, who was instructing by carefully demonstrating and marking carefully and deliberately on the lines on the chalkboard. I picked up my pencil and began marking on the lines on my paper, trying very carefully to replicate the teacher's actions. As I glanced at the other students, I noticed closeby students holding the pencil with their right hand and copying the teacher's actions. I had instinctively picked up my pencil with my left hand. Noticing how other students were holding their pencils, I tried to appear inconspicuous while learning to write the written symbols which would make up the basis of life-long written communication. Why was I not using my right hand to hold the pencil? Why? Does it matter? As someone later in life told me, it doesn't matter, just learn to do it the right way. I guess it doesn't matter much to some people though it is usually right-handed people who would say this to me. After all, what matters is getting the job or task done. Just compromise – do your best, or find a job more suited to your "liking". Then again, maybe it did matter!

Thesis:

In a system that I believe is largely designed by and for left-brain dominance, right-handed individuals, there is evidence in nature that the uniqueness of right-brain dominance in many of whom exhibit left-handedness, is by design. Due to two brain hemispheres with innate differences and characteristics, I believe there has to be a design with purpose (Creator). This book is written to give a broad overview of life as a leftie – with some details to illustrate my observations and thinking from my personal experience. I believe the differences in brain dominance hemispheres contribute to genetic combinations of traits which may result in different perspectives, personality characteristics, temperament, skillset, abilities, etc.... Feedback and perception from an individual's senses and the involvement of both hemispheres is necessary for efficient processing of information, whichever hemisphere is dominant. Building upon an individual's innate nature, there may be proactive and reactive nurturing which may enhance and influence opportunities and life events. Therefore the learner who has free will to learning and awareness through education and programs may experience encouragement and enlightenment to accomplish their life's goals.

Why write another book, when the libraries are full of books of all types, formats, media, and sizes? My main reason for writing this particular book is to encourage left handers and enlighten others through imparting my 74 years of experience in a very "limited edition" and to give my perspective on left-handedness in a mostly right-handed world.

I do not claim to have all the answers, only that I am on a knowledge adventure, discovering interesting and helpful information. I want to always be a learner, seeking, observing and experiencing, hopefully recognizing opportunities to help others along the way.

How to best experience use of this book:

To get the best meaning and understanding of purpose of this book, please visit websites referenced when reading through this book to obtain information and also read the Addendum Notes Sections A through J in the back of the book.

I believe there are several types of left-handers:

1. **Dominately left-handed** – those who are right brain, left eye, left ear, left-hand (close to 100%)
2. **Predominantly left-handed**, but in varying degrees do some things right-handed, almost to the point of being left-brain dominant, and vice versa, predominantly right-handed, but in varying degrees do some things left-handed almost to the point of being right-brain dominant; a few may be ambidextrous.
3. **Switched** - left-handers who became right-handers mostly for writing due to early re-training and intervention (perhaps meaningful parental, educational, or cultural pressure; however brain processes remain right brain dominant.) Perhaps depending on how much influential nuances and intricacies occurred in intellectual development before the re-training became the focus, they may be only subliminally aware or not aware at all that they are naturally left-handed. Or even, DENIERS who try to pass themselves off as right-handers.
4. **Circumstantially left-handed due to a life-altering event** - Right-handers who became left-handers due to some life changing event, perhaps an accident or medical issue causing loss of the right hand or limb. (Of course, this could also happen causing a left-hander to become right-handed).

I also believe there has been discrimination against left-handers throughout world history. I have experienced some stigmatization, but not physically, such as some have had their left hand rapped or tied to their chair or behind their back to ensure they get the message to use the right-hand. Left-handed individuals may be more aware of handedness than right-handed individuals due to the need to accommodate the difference.

I believe some people are more creative or adaptive by nature or personality, but left-handers in general are "forced" to become creative, for they have to learn to adapt in this right-handed world.

Interesting Information

Following is some information I discovered while researching:

It seems society now is more cognizant of left-handers, however they are still sometimes misunderstood and generally not accommodated with appropriate things like tools, equipment, school desks.

This new level of left-handed awareness may have increased due to professional sports prominence with mass media coverage. There may be more realization of the advantage when dominant left-handers are playing sports such as baseball, football, basketball, golf, volley ball. Video captures movements and actions, with the ability to watch, slow down, comment, and replay. The sportscasters give viewers up-close views and can call attention to every move made in certain sporting events.

Perhaps the publicized and professional sports, with its countless millions of fans has been the single greatest societal change that has (unintentionally) made the greatest leap toward the acceptance and appreciation of lefties in society.

LEFT HEMISPHERE OR RIGHT HEMISPHERE?

What? Dominance Difference? .... Why?

I became aware at a very young age that life can be confusing - - when repeatedly told I was not using the right hand when doing certain tasks. This was later confirmed when I began attending school and became aware that not everyone was writing with their left hand. I was not like everyone else around me.

Also, over the years I have become aware that many times I speak in allegories and innuendos – not direct and to the point like many people have the ability to do. I tend to skip over some "intermediate" comment/steps and state directly my "summary" conclusion, leaving the person listening wondering why I stated what I said or what is the point? I think what I had said gives enough facts and evidence that whoever is listening could not reach any other than the same "summary conclusion" other than what I had concluded. But this does not seem to always be the case, since they ask follow up questions or ask for more information from me.

Transitional Information Exchange in the Brain Hemispheres?

I am wondering if this verbal communication manner and/or transitional information exchange is why I sometimes have physical exhaustion, that it may be due to mental exhaustion or fatigue as the information transitions through the dominant brain to the opposite side and depending on how familiar the information is to me, how much mental effort has to be exerted to process and weigh options or decisions for absorbing the information.

This transitional information exchange may be part of the communication occurrence, and may be how both left and right-handers must mentally process information.

PERSONALITY TESTS AND TEMPERAMENT TESTS

There are some personality tests and temperament tests available on the internet, some at no charge. These may help you identify your personality type. One personality type may be quite different from another. I have noticed that the results of the test may be self-informative. However; there may be other individuals close to you or those you come in contact with who view the person's personality as being different than what is reflected in the tests.

In some respects, I think personality and temperament tests may be taken with a pinch of salt, considering the results while keeping in mind a degree of skepticism about its truth. These tests may be used as a way to know yourself better. And, some tests may show your interests, strengths, weaknesses, gifts or talents. These may go as far as to help make some decisions in life easier; for example, matching personalities with career paths and goals in life.

WHICH HAND TO WRITE WITH?

TESTS FOR HANDEDNESS

Some of these tests can be found by searching the internet. I came across an interesting test recently in an older book that I have referenced in the Addendum Notes, for anyone who wishes to discover more about handedness.

Some left-handers have been switched from left- to right-handedness by a family member or someone's intervention early in their life due to feelings that there is a right hand advantage. Then, some may think they are "cured" from being right brain, left-handed! (my attempt at humor) However, there may be an added skillset of using the right hand for handwriting.

There are others who have experienced life as a right hander and due to some life changing event have had to become left-handed - or the reverse. These individuals may have become aware of the biases against handedness in tools, cooking utensils, life skills, because they once had hand dominance but now have no choice but to go on through life using the other hand.

DYSLEXIA – MORE RIGHT BRAIN PERCENTAGE?

Sometimes those who consider themselves to have some form of dyslexia, (such as myself - "directionally challenged") have a difficult time reading maps, or following written directions. Help to overcome my directional challenges can include having landmarks for guidance, memorizing routes and never deviating from them, and leaving for a destination long enough to compensate for getting lost.

Knowing that dyslexia may be behind the confusion with direction and that there may be others with the same challenges like this can help alleviate negative self-talk.

Dyslexic Brain and relation to Whole Brain Thinking

Video information about the Dyslexic Brain from the internet are giving information that scientific and academic researchers are currently providing.

Please take a moment to check out internet information including these videos:

'The Dyslexic Brain – Wired for Whole Brain Thinking'

'How a Dyslexic Brain Works – A Simple Demonstration' on YouTube

'The True Gifts of a Dyslexic Mind' – TEDxMarthas Vineyard – an inspirational talk by Dean Bragonier

I can totally relate to the demonstration on 'How a Dyslexic Brain Works.' I see connections between the card "pile", searching for a particular card, and in the process finding previously meaningful or forgotten cards (color, design, category). I see comparing similarities, contrasts, and possibly re-using or applying the "card" to a different situation. With respect to problem solving, I personally relate to my feeling of "searching" for a proverbial particular needle in the haystack, finally finding the needle, then continuing to search for the thread, finally finding the right (or suitable substitution) thread and then being able to put the two (needle and thread together, figuratively) to accomplish something meaningful or useful. Of course, this sometimes takes time and for me personally, sometimes I wake up from sleep with the "puzzle" solved. I have learned when this happens, go ahead and get up, find a pen and paper, and write it down. Otherwise, I toss and turn trying not to forget what I need to remember, and even then, the next day sometimes I cannot recall quickly what the "puzzle" solution was. Better for me to get up and write it down.

This video can also confirm the difference of opinion regarding decisions required with a statement as simple as "It's time to clean your room." To one person, that request may mean emptymost everything out of the room, dust and vacuum, and then place like kind items in an orderly fashion on shelves or desks, hang and arrange clean items in the closet, etc. To another person, that request may simply mean remove empty and dirty food containers, sort out and do the laundry. My decision-making when going through the "haystack" pile of a disorganized, disoriented task would include things like "Keep", "Donate", "Decide Later", "Discard", "Yard Sale", "Sell online", etc. Sometimes the process of deciding is made one item at a time. If I am thinking "efficiently", I may look at everything with the motive of gathering up all of the "Donate" items, then maybe the "Discard" items, and so on throughout the task. The key for me is "FOCUS" and keep on task until finished! Whether left-handed or right-handed, sometimes daunting tasks challenge us through the phases of simply starting, and staying with it until wrapping it up at the end.

The video "The True Gifts of a Dyslexic Mind" is very comforting and encouraging information. I think there is finally recognition and acknowledgement of the value of people who think differently. We are each a unique individual with many factors involved including the proverbial question: Is it Nature or Nurture (or a mixture of both)? However, I think there is a missing portion of the presentation - - I think handedness could possibly be related to dyslexia. There does not seem to be any cognizant awareness of left-handedness currently being addressed. Maybe it is subliminally being down played, hoping that the whole-brain agenda will eventually "gene pool" us lefties into conforming and eventually fading out of existence. But, just looking around, there are lefties in existence, and there have been for ages!

"In this inspiring talk advocate and educator Dean Bragonier offers a different take on Dyslexia. By looking at the unique mindset of dyslexics as a strength, Dean reframes a perceived weakness as a powerful tool and teaches us all an important lesson about the power of an open mind and an open heart." Published Nov. 24, 2015

I could be wrong since research here may be a work in progress, but …my "Note to Observers"

I think some "right brain wired left-handers" display observable dyslexic actions.

If you know of a child or someone who has a child who displays any seemingly dyslexic observable actions consider this interesting research discovered from internet information taken from Web MD 1/4/17. Some exams and tests may be done when it seems appropriate. It is diagnosed (by a team of professionals) when:

- There is evidence of a severe reading problem
- The problem is not due to low intelligence, a visual or hearing deficit or other physical conditions, or a lack of educational opportunity.
- A single test can't diagnose dyslexia. Rather, your doctor or a school professional (such as a reading specialist) will ask you what sign of dyslexia you and your child's teachers have seen. He or she will ask your child questions too.

- Reading tests and other types of assessments may be done to help find out about your child's skills. For example tests may include those that focus on your child's learning style, language and problem-solving skills, and intelligence quotient (IQ).
- Typically children with dyslexia are very bright, although reading will probably continue to be a challenge throughout life. The earlier dyslexia is recognized and addressed, the greater the chance that your child will learn to read at his or her highest possible level.
- Encouraging and supporting your child while staying involved in his or her education are the key factors.
- Helping children with coping strategies as they advance in school will also help. Although extra effort and dedication are required, often children with dyslexia are able to contend with this disability and succeed in academics and other areas.
- Most people think dyslexia is a condition that involves reading from right to left and reversing words and letters. While some people with dyslexia do have these patterns, they are not the most common or most important characteristics of dyslexia. Experts say dyslexia has little to do with recognizing the visual form of words; rather, the brains of people with dyslexia are wired differently. This difference makes it difficult to break the letters of written words into the distinct sounds (or phonemes) of their language, a capability called phonological awareness.
- Dyslexia can occur at any level of intellectual ability. Sometimes children with dyslexia appear to their teachers and parents to lack motivation or not be trying hard enough. Dyslexia may be accompanied by—but is not a result of—lack of motivation, emotional or behavioral problems, and sensory impairment.
- A more positive view of dyslexia describes people with dyslexia as visual, multidimensional thinkers who are intuitive, highly creative, and excel at hands-on learning. Many people with dyslexia shine in the arts, creativity, design, computers, and lateral thinking.

(The excerpt ABOVE is from Web MD.com/children, understanding-dyslexia-basics) (What is dyslexia?)

What I think!

Some people may not be diagnosed with dyslexia as children, and for one reason or another, they may be diagnosed later when they are adults.

Maybe the concept of "dyslexia" has become a norm label to include left-handedness, even though those "left-handed" labels are not used. May be that left-handed people have a higher rate of dyslexia, and it may be that the structure of the brain and thinking, sometimes manifests results in left-handedness. And I also wonder if the changing from left to right-handedness is to reduce the stress and "stigma" of being different. The person may be aware or only subliminally aware of that change which was done to minimize or diminish the left-handed use in order to better assimilate with the majority in the right-handed world.

It seems the term left-handed is not used because perhaps the goal is now "whole brain"? However, I am not sure this total inclusion will succeed in causing left-handers to conform. After all, there are the identifiable cerebral hemispheres of the left brain and the right brain (two distinct halves joined by the corpus callosum which is responsible for transmitting neural messages between both the right and the left hemispheres).

A little about Leftie Traits

TRAITS AND EXPLANATIONS LIST I garnered according to A Left-Handed History of the World by Ed Wright.

Exemplifying characteristics have been exhibited by lefties throughout history, from the noblest status to the common person:

Intuitive

Empathetic

Visual spatial ability

Visual spatial learning styles - often referred to as the spatial learning style, is a way of **learning** in which information is associated with images.

Lateral thinking Author's note: to think "outside the box" is more than critical thinking (and who is to say - - maybe there never was a box).

An example of out of the box thinking that I came across in reading and researching was of someone who when being confronted with a rising river quickly converted a tent into a raft to float down the river.

As defined by WikiLeaks on the free internet dictionary:

Lateral thinking in (Psychology) a way of solving problems by rejecting traditional methods and employing unorthodox and apparently illogical means.

Lateral thinking is solving problems through an indirect and creative approach, using reasoning that is not immediately obvious and involving ideas that may not be obtainable by using only traditional step-by-step logic.[1] The term was promulgated in 1967 by Edward de Bono. He cites as an example the Judgment of Solomon, where King Solomon resolves a dispute over the parentage of a child by calling for the child to be cut in half, and making his judgment according to the reactions that this order receives.[2]

Strong emotions, could be Emotionally Hot Tempered (author's note: - even directed at self when you make a mistake or life doesn't go as expected or your "buttons are pushed") or you are teased or criticized or become frustrated at not doing things the "right" way.

Solitary

Iconoclastic

Self-Taught

Experimental – "what if" then try it out.

Author's note: Imaginative – quickly see beyond a situation, whether in reality or visualization

(Unable to contact publisher about copyright permission) Ed Wright, "A Left-Handed History of the World, first published in 2007 by Pier 9, an imprint of Murdoch Books Pty Limited ISBN 978:7419605302. (updated with new revision in 2011)

A quote I came across while surfing the internet: "Logic will get you from A to B: imagination will take you everywhere."

PART ONE

AUTHOR'S PERSPECTIVE A LITTLE FRIENDLY ADVICE

CHAPTER 1

Don't Panic – Remain Calm!

Here's some advice I would offer to you if you internalize that you may be right brain dominant and if you become surprised that you may be (or are) a natural or switched leftie, or if you have an experience or issue due to handedness and think it is affecting you negatively, just acquire knowledge from observing, reading informational books, studying, listening to music, etc. Find a way to "return to reality" that works for you – maybe have a cup of coffee or tea to enjoy, or go for a walk, talk to a friend. One of my most favorite things to do each morning is to step outside to thank God for another day. I especially like to be observant of the birds flying in the heavens. I am reminded of the song, "His eye is on the sparrow" and I know He watches me.

If you have felt that you are a disadvantaged left-hander in a right-hander situation... don't panic. Remember there have been some great achievements by lefties, from historical times in the past ages of Europe to more recent times including Benjamin Franklin: printer, journalist, inventor, philosopher, advocate of civic development and organization, diplomat assisting with treaties involving other countries. In addition, he was the first Postmaster General who was key in developing the United States Postal Service. As a founding member of the Constitutional Convention in 1787, he helped shape our constitution. And I read that his last public act was signing a memorial to Congress, asking for the abolishment of slavery. His influence has had a significant, lasting impact in our country and world. So, remember that left-handers from all walks of life have made many contributions (maybe just getting through a challenge with grace and a good attitude!) and have shaped and continue to shape our world.

I was researching the topic of International Left Handers Day and found interesting reading on Wikipedia. This reminded me that some information I have read or heard about suggests left-handedness has been portrayed as sinister. Maybe this is remnant of a time in history when superstitions abounded (perhaps due to knowledge unaware).

However, we can openly discuss this topic as it is likely to come up, as happened recently in a conversation my daughter relayed to me. She was talking with a friend and it came up in conversation that the friend is left-handed. Immediately in the discussion, the friend asked her if she knew it was once common for people to believe that left-handed people were sinister. My right-handed daughter was surprised that her friend brought this up because she believes the prevailing thought today would go against thinking that one was sinister due to an innate physical genetic trait. The friend is a civil engineer by profession and made the statement that left-handed people have also been known to be very smart! My thoughts regarding this conversation is that God designed us to be free-willed. We can pursue choices of good or evil, as we learn in the Bible book of Galatians Chapter 5:14-25. I like to remember that the Holy Spirit is greater than the non-holy spirit that is in the world. (1 John Chapter 4:4).

In an attempt to alleviate a situation, some may be hoping that by moving somewhere else, or surrounding themselves by others, life will change. However, I am reminded of that old saying, "Wherever I go, there I am." Don't go too far out into "left field." Come back to reality! It's going to be OK! You are not alone…

Observing some prominent people writing, eating, or using their left hand instead of the right hand can really bring awareness and realization of handedness in society.

Left handers may be aware of left-handedness as much or more than being aware of being color-blind or having some other physical challenge.

Some may think left-handers should organize due to a need for publicity and public relations, but I think many lefties are independent and do not feel a need to organize. However, when I notice another left-hander I like to reach out to them and meet them.

CHAPTER 2

About Judging Others

Although some people may not believe this, I think and have become aware that at some point in life, a lefty becomes aware of being different and thinking differently. I have felt that some were judging my left-handed actions, not accepting the idea that characteristics of left-handed individuals are that they seem independent, and look at the world with a different view. The brain thought processes are different. Sometimes I didn't realize that I had an issue until later when some circumstance or event identified that I have a different perspective. When I review the characteristics previously mentioned as left-hander's exemplifying characteristics or traits, I recall being called names (lazy, clumsy, not grasping reality and the correct way to do something.)

An example of looking awkward was when asked to help with the punchbowl at a party. I looked awkward due to pouring punchbowl punch into a cup from a ladle. If I poured using my right hand it looked awkward because I normally would use my left hand. If I poured using my left hand, there was either no pouring spout on the ladle and the punch did not pour right, or if I poured from the spout on the ladle, it was on the back side of the ladle. Either way, the pouring looked awkward, because Plan A pouring using the right hand did not work easily and Plan B looked even more so.

Recently I had the experience of using an electric long-handled pole saw to prune fruit trees. I quickly became aware of right-handed design when I discovered in addition to the trigger in the front part of the saw motor where the handle is, there is also a button on the left side of the handle. Both had to be simultaneously used in order to activate the saw blade. I finally used both hands on the saw and got the branches cut.

I recently came across a publication at the library stating that right brain/ left brain is a "Myth". The question I ask is, "Then, why am I writing with my left hand, and why do I observe others who are writing with their right hand?" While at a public meeting recently, there was a sign-in attendance sheet. As I was signing in, someone in line behind me asked "Do they let left-handed people use the pen?" After finishing signing in, I looked around, and several people behind me in the line were looking at me. The person who said that was probably joking, and may have been a left-hander himself or knew of left-handers. Be careful if talking against or criticizing what you do not know about or understand – try to understand another point of view first. It has been said, seek to understand others, and hopefully they will seek to understand you!

Decisions—Distractions—Criticism (instead of Encouragement)—Obstructions

Subliminal vs deliberate list-oriented focused Decision Making!!

Again, I agree with the previously referenced video regarding the dyslectic brain, particularly the "How a Dyslexic Brain Works – A Simple Demonstration".

Due to the observed sometimes disadvantage in a right-handed environment, even my mother would sometimes comment that I needed help. Many times, I felt like I was resorting to "Plan B" because "Plan A" demonstrated through my experience didn't work!

I have come to realize a way to describe my decision making tasks is like the crimp ribbon candy at Christmastime.

My "Decision-making" documented and modeled!

Plan A

Winding toward the right crimp a little until a decision-challenge of something not working the right way (seemingly figuratively speaking "confronting an obstruction"), then when sometimes realizing a different option may work better, winding back toward the left crimp until confronting another challenge, possibly a decision needs to quickly be made, then re-analyzing the situation and winding back to the right, etc. until finally ...voil'a... a solution and persistance resulting in ... **Plan B**! the task or project completion!

A challenge (or seemingly something impeding my continuing to focus on the task albeit sometimes brief) requires a credible focus and maybe analysis of decision(s) which enables the turning back towards the other direction to solve the "impediment" of how to do something or obtain the end result. "Figuring out" what to do is another name I have given it. Sometimes there is only one fold or crimp, but sometimes several or many folds until I have a satisfactory plan to accomplish the result, which is Plan B to me. I may definitely identify with crimp ribbon candy differently than some. (ha)

One example is when there is a room to be rearranged or a clean up task to be done, I can identify with the demonstration video cards that are the unorganized pile. It helps me to stay focused on the tasks and have sorting categories, labeled "Keep", "Needs attention", "Donation box", "Discard", "Sell", …"Decide Later". The Decide Later category may be considered PROCRASTINATION by some people; however, if there are multiple options to explore, a final decision or completion of the project or task may be pushed out until a later time. Sometimes I ask for help, break up the process into smaller steps and achievements, delegate or re-prioritize and decide to do something else for awhile. When embarking on tasks, whether large or small, sometimes I get overwhelmed. The tasks need to get done, and there may be other ways to the "mountaintop" although some ways are more meandering than direct.

I identify my deliberate committed plan of attack on some task I have procrastinated over or definitely consider "not my favorite kind of task" and then decide on the best way for me to proceed. I may write down:

Step 1
Step 2
Step 3, etc.

This eliminates my having to constantly think of the next step in the process to finish the task and achieve the revered feeling of completion of a task or project. Sometimes, I reassess the order of the steps hoping for more time or energy efficiency to complete the task.

Another example I can provide is that of driving in complex unfamiliar territory, it can take me an hour or more to arrive at a 15 minute destination. If I have driving directions or a map, I may locate which road, but then turn the opposite direction of where I need to turn. I also try to memorize and be cognizant of landmarks or road marks, and even then if there is a different sign (i.e. yard sign or traffic sign) it looks unfamiliar and I may not turn the right direction. I always have to be aware and then be prepared to turn around (depending on road conditions, this could be a mile or more before it is possible to turn around.) Maybe this is why everyday seems 'new' when I look around – in my mind's eye it is 'new'!

Some of my Personal Experiences and Anecdotes with Lefties and Left-Handedness:

Some responses to comments that I have made to other lefties is that of:

- "We think differently."
- A person to whom I commented that he was another leftie, reached across the desk we were seated at, and simply shook my hand! (Invisible, silent comaraderie, understanding!)
- Another sweet lady, who is a little older than I, said when she was in school in the 1930's, her teacher tied her left hand to the desk which was as at that time arranged in a row of three desks (right-handed desks). This was to train her to write correctly with her right hand. When recess came, all the students hurried out, but she remained with her left hand tied to the desk.
- One of my granddaughters recently mentioned that her class received new desks at school, and they were all right hand desks with a small writing area. Reflecting on my own early school years and possibly subliminal frustration with being disadvantaged as a left hander, I immediately felt empathy for my granddaughter. But she had a positive attitude and solution: she told me, "Grandma, it's OK. All I have to do is turn toward the right side of the desk, turn my paper, and it works!" Yaaa for inventiveness that lefties contrive. By this, my granddaughter has proven to understand her disadvantage – but has learned to be adaptive. She is another leftie who has figured out Plan B, because Plan A obviously doesn't work. Others in the class are probably wondering, why doesn't she just use the desk the right way?
- But, don't judge - - the school probably has budget priorities! Think how much may have been saved in desks not having to be special ordered. Ha

- Someone I relayed this story to stated, maybe your granddaughter should withdraw from that school and enroll in a school where there are left-handers!
- Another left-handed individual I came across stated that her mother had someone design a left-arm support to use at school when there were no left-handed desks. She said she used it all through high school.
- Someone else I came across stated that her mother in law went to school at a time when the teacher who had a left-handed student deemed it necessary to change and thus discipline the student with a smack from a ruler on top of the "incorrect hand" use.
- I was recently attending a class and when signing in at the registration table, someone in line behind me said "Do they let left handers use the pen?" (probably was a left-handed individual or knew someone who is left-handed)
- A left-handed high school student who was graduating at the end of the school year, when learning I was writing this book, said to me "Finally, someone understands!"
- I was asked to include in this book the fact that the LEFT hand is always on top when learning the proper way to play a recorder. Maybe the recorder was invented by a left hander!
- A Lutherier (repairer of stringed instruments) believes that left handers have an advantage in playing the guitar. The chords are played using the left fingertips, while the right hand is used to pick or strum across the strings. There are some who believe a guitar designed for a left hander (reversed design from most guitars) is needed; however the individual playing the instrument may then need to also be re-taught or the method of playing re-thought.
- Some of my personal hobby experience includes reading instructions (and probably reversing) for sewing and crocheting. I have had some strange and interesting results!

A right-handed mother never gave thought to what her left-handed daughter went through at school until she homeschooled her in the 7th grade. The mother witnessed how the daughter would curve her left hand to write and how her left hand did not rest on the page because it had to rest on the metal spiral of the notebook, and then her hand moved across the un-dry ink or pencil lead marks on the page.

An interesting story in *The Left Hander's Handbook* listed in the Addendum, relayed that "In the public and church-run schools of America's towns and cities however, teachers encouraged students to write with their right hands: many are the stories of staunch lefties who had their knuckles rapped, or worse. But at the turn of this century, Americans began to do research on the education of the left-handed. Enlightened parents saw to it that their children were not forced to switch. The author Jessamyn West, born in Indiana in 1902, had such parents. She has related that she went to school in the days when teachers did not allow left-handed penmanship- even to the extent of tying the left arm of students behind their back, until they learned to write 'correctly.' West's parents came to her rescue. 'My mother sent me to school with a note saying, 'God intended this child to use her left hand,' she has recalled. So the teacher let me alone. I don't think she was afraid to go against my mother, but she wasn't going to go against God." (pg. 31)

Plight as a member of a peculiar minority

Some humorous insight can be gained by reading an excerpt article from "Life on the Left" depicting sometimes subliminal decisions which must be made due to left handers adapting to living in the right-handed world.

It is from a book of required reading for a creative writing class from an obviously left-handed imaginative perspective of the writer. It related the disadvantages using light (and slightly dry) humor. Many left-handers would likely identify with some of the incidents mentioned in the article! It is included in the Addendum Notes section in the back of the book – please take a few moments to read it to increase your left-hander plight-knowledge! (Writing: Craft and Art by William L. Rivers)

My Benefit of a LEFT-Handed desk!

Recently, I attended a workshop about fraud and security precautions for senior citizens, which was held at a nearby college. One of the breakout sessions was in a classroom with student desks to use during the 45-minute long session. What a pleasant surprise and instant choice - - most of the chairs had a right-handed top but at the end of the front row, there were two LEFT-handed desks! It was wonderful to sit comfortably, able to rest my left arm while taking notes during the session. WOW, it was great to be acknowledged and provided a comfortable working space. I basked in the cognizance of a comfortable working space. No more trying to make-do while writing at a right-hand desk. At the left-hand desk, I could concentrate on listening to the speaker and taking notes on the subject matter!

Rightie who became a Leftie!

I know a very special person who used to be a rightie until one day a horrific electrical accident resulted in his becoming left-handed. It is an exceptionally amazing story that after amputation of the right hand and arm below the elbow, he endured physical therapy and was eventually able to return to his plumbing profession, by using leverage and pulley concepts to help him complete his work tasks.

This special person's daily reward at the end of the workday, is coming home to a loving and supportive family. Any given day could include climbing under houses, removing plumbing or remodeling and installing new fixtures, inspecting and researching to give quotes. Those who know him have noted that he is a one-armed man with the work ethic of three men at one time. He is meticulous in his approach to work, making customers happy while earning a living and providing for his family. He stated to me that he is surprised at how positive and patient his approach to life is. I think it is a "God thing."

Reverse Transitional Exchange?

And in interviewing him, he mentioned that after about 20 years of becoming left-handed, he has noticed that some of the letters and numbers he is required to write are reversed, as in dyslexic. I am wondering if the use of the left hand in this type of situation is retracting back to cause the right brain to become more dominate than in the previous status of being left brain, right-handed. The challenge of forevermore using the previously left-dominant brain may now be forced in the realm of right-dominant brain. This change may cause gloomy or threatening feelings of despair and discouragement for an uncertain future and may cause reaching out and searching for help to cope with a changing life situation. Help could come through family, friends, community, God, even including a loyal pet companion or work pet.

The renowned King David of old, in the Bible book of Psalms 34:4 states: "I sought the Lord, and He heard me, and delivered me from all my fears."

Work buddy – Scout, taking a respite.

Compassion and Consideration

How about a little compassion and/or consideration that a left-hander may have a different brain structure and thought processes, as discovered in my research. (The Left Handers' Handbook, pg 84):

Instead of *judging* and/or calling a leftie:

Stubborn, rebellious, different, lazy, slow (I think due to the decision-making deliberation process), plodding, skeptical, or socially maladjusted.

Just may be they are:

Independent, although asking overtly or covertly for assistance
Willing to go it alone
Original
Thoughtful
Persistent
Questioning
and
Nonconformist (The Left Handers' Handbook pg 84)

Sooooo, my personal feeling is: we need to try not to judge or criticize others when they make or say things against us lefties for appearing different. Forgive them. (Remember to forgive yourself also.) If someone appears to think more highly or intelligently of themselves, I am reminded that even the most intelligent individual or genius probably has some weakness(s), because after all, we are all human and if thinking someone is less of a "genius", even that individual has some God given, unique strength(s) or abilities.

CHAPTER 3

Accentuate the Positive

One's attitude makes the difference!

People with challenges or disabilities may have tended to become angry, frustrated, hurt…by others and society who seemingly de-value them. Left-handedness is not a disability – but in this mostly right-handed world it has been and is sometimes a disadvantage. You may or may not agree, but this has been my personal experience.

An ordinary leftie could become a game changer! If someone is critical or demeans you because of your left-handedness and those traits, don't condemn or be too hard on yourself for being different. Some have tried to pass themselves off as being righties – because of society's rightie bias against lefties. They may believe they have "cured" themselves of left-handedness simply because they have been taught to write using the right hand. However, learning to write with the right hand may be an additional skill training to their advantage! So oftentimes, the challenges left-handers face can lead to having more skills and abilities. And, as I have observed, right-handers may have challenges too.

My Personal Three Steps to Resolving My Internal Conflict or Stress Toward Positive Thinking

Sometimes I have felt that there were personal name-calling against me that I did not deserve, whether intentional or not. Someone doing things or instructing you and not acknowledging the left hand difference, can cause conflict in life. When you face situations or occasions that cause stress, first recognize the stressful situation; second, identify your typical reaction; and third, identify steps to try to reconcile your typical reaction (know yourself!) choice:

Step 1: Recognize the stressful situation

Step 2: Identify your typical reaction

- Anger
- Feeling of Rejection
- Jealousy
- Hatred
- Strife
- Dissension
- Denial
- Stumble through it
- Communicate verbally (or nonverbally)
- Try Avoidance of hurtful or uncomfortable situation
- Other? Reason or discuss the situation

Step 3: Breathe Deeply, Count to 10 and think positively OUTSIDE THE BOX!

See and appreciate the sometimes humor in the "different thinking" or viewing the world through different eyes. Don't be critical of those who think differently from you.

By being a learner searching for knowledge and wisdom, some background information from the Bible informs us that there is always conflict between the negative occurrences and the choice of better ways of dealing with situations which cause conflict.

If we are needing help in a situation, the Bible book of Hebrews says that there could be angels unaware. Sometimes they appear and we may interact with them without knowing they are angels intervening. We are blessed and enriched many times over by their presence. It can be more than coincidence in our lives!

Don't be jealous that someone is being blessed and you feel that you are not: be appreciative and thankful to/for them.

Some positive reactions and actions to choose from could be:

Accept guidance and direction from the principles in the Bible and the indwelling Holy Spirit (not always the emotion-directed feelings). If you ask for wisdom, God gives liberally. James 5:2-5

Ask God for guidance in ways to communicate. God can give you the words and ways to make them useful and meaningful in life. Luke 12:1-12 Remember words aren't the only way to communicate.

Forgive yourself, forgive others. Matthew 6:9-12

Ask for, and accept help from someone if needed. And reciprocate if you can help someone else.

Value Yourself

Ask and trust God to direct your skills and knowledge. I could easily have become in a discard/rejected feeling. At one point in my life, I found myself needing to go back to work after being a homemaker for some years while my children were young. I was told, no need to apply, I would not get hired. I decided to go ahead and apply, and was hired due to some skills which I had acquired in school earlier in my academic years (shorthand, typing at above average speed).

If an individual does not have the convenient gift of "gab" (articulate, instantaneous, convenient expression) that does not mean that individual has no value.

If you are at a low point in life, recognize a kind word could represent the difference between the world of negativity and the world of positivity.

I would say, pick yourself up, assess your goals in life (you may need someone and/or professional experience to help with goals), and start all over again.

Find something good to be thankful for in every day.

Wake Up the Body through Movement

From personal experience, I have experienced less energy, and even "writer's block" until I begin doing something involving physical activity. I think whatever brain dominance tendency, movement can help. In my research, there appears to be various coordinated activities to help get the cross movement "energy flowing", maybe this bridges between the right brain and the left brain. There has been research and resultant activities for training and even certification as trainers offered by various programs in cross movements (right hand, left side of body, and left hand, right side of body movements), to improve the energy flow within the body.

Kinesiology Muscle Testing and Muscle Response

Along the adventure of researching and discovery, here is some information to ponder about kinesiology.

As defined on Wisegeek.com., kinesiology is the scientific study of the body's movements. Applied kinesiology, or muscle testing, is a branch within alternative medicine that manual tests the muscles' function and uses those results to determine the overall health of the body. Because muscle testing is not deeply rooted in traditional notions of science, it has not gone without criticism.

Manual muscle testing is a simple procedure with potentially complex implications. Like acupuncture, it is a derivative of Chinese medicine, and therefore ties into a belief that the body is governed by a network of meridians that convey energy. Despite its recent rise in popularity, muscle testing is not new, having first been introduced into western culture in the early 20th century. It is related to, and is also known as, applied kinesiology which is generally said to have been developed by chiropractor, George Goodheart in the 1960s.

The International College of Applied Kinesiology (ICAK) has established an "operational definition" for manual muscle testing. It essentially defines the test as a tool to evaluate how the nervous system helps the muscles adapt to the changing pressure it receives by the examiner. A qualified examiner of a muscle test, therefore, should be properly educated in muscle function and have had proper training in anatomy, physiology, and neurology. Manual muscle testing, ICAK contends, is not only science, but art as well.

My right-handed daughter discovered she was challenged during group fitness classes when the instructor would call out the movements. Instead of quitting, she kept at it and improved the listening and movement coordination. Coincidentally, as the group fitness classes became easier mentally and physically, she recalled that her studies in college improved and she was often surprised to receive the highest grade in the class. She attributed her focus concentration, and memory skills improvement from the fitness classes to the improvement in her academic classes. This is her experience and her insight – and perhaps topic research can document the facts!

Consider Available Education and Programs in Preparation for Life's Obligations

Life Skills Program

I believe both left brain dominant and right brain dominant individuals may at times benefit from helpful education - some may be community based living programs or through social programs. These programs may be of special interest to some individuals who feel homeless, helpless, hopeless and are interested in a hand-up to help identify and help accomplish goals.

If you wish to acquire more help and professional-type development, do some research of programs offered and available, such as:

- Education Soft Skills Work Ethic Decision Making
- Problem Solving

- Creative Thinking
- Critical Thinking
- Effective Communication
- Interpersonal Relationships
- Self Awareness and Mindfulness
- Assertiveness
- Empathy for and Helping Others
- Equanimity
- Coping with Stress, Trauma and Loss
- Resilience

(Reference Life Skills Program in the Addendum Notes which gives additional information)

Time Management and Prioritizing

One area that I personally find very important is planning out the necessary things I need to accomplish daily with a written job list. This helps me stay on task (even though occasionally things do get pushed forward to another day.) A monthly calendar updated each month with some continuity month-to-month reminders is a necessity for me. There are some time management aids and training I have had throughout my life and probably is the reason I am feeling that I can look back over my life breathing a sigh of relief. Of course there are things in hindsight I learned from and would have done differently, as possibly most people could identify with.

Ergonomics

The subject of ergonomics appeals to me because of making life better for us. Years ago, the term ergonomics may have been an unfamiliar word. Today, more people are familiar with ergonomics; Ergonomics can roughly be defined as the study of people in their working environment. More specifically, an ergonomist designs the work area for a worker, to eliminate or minimize discomfort or injury risk.

Left-handed ergonomics is available for students and employees depending on the situation. I personally have adapted and do not seek out left-handed designs, but I do know those who find things, such as computer keyboards, make a difference.

Be the Best You Can Be

When wanting to improve in an area, I know that practice helps! Sometimes visualization techniques in which you can see yourself doing what you want to do helps. Concentration and perseverance sometimes is necessary depending on whether or not you are determined to succeed at accomplishing the task.

When I was younger, I was interested in learning to crochet. However, the person willing to teach me was right-handed. I watched and practiced right-handed but decided that was not working for me. So I kept watching the way the yarn was held and the movements of the crochet needle, then experimented until I was able to bring the yarn loop through to complete a stitch, eventually making the basic chain stitch. Over the years, I made many things for home décor, gifts, clothing, etc. Sometimes when following instructions to make something, it was easier to look at the finished picture or drawing than to interpret the instructions. And, I have to admit sometimes the result was creative and humorous, at times resulting in unraveling the stitches and starting over! Some of the sewing and craftwork was from economic necessity when these items were not so readily accessible and affordable as they are today; and there is that old saying, "necessity is the mother of invention."

And again, there is that saying,"If life hands you lemons, make lemonade!" It may be that the skills you have are brilliant in some areas more than in some other areas.

I once heard someone say the epithet on a tombstone was,"She did the best she could, with what she had." Sounds like a good one – I want that one as my memorial too. And I always remember, do my best, ask God to do the rest.

***

PART TWO

ACKNOWLEDGING

CHAPTER 4

Acknowledge the Difference!

There can be successes!

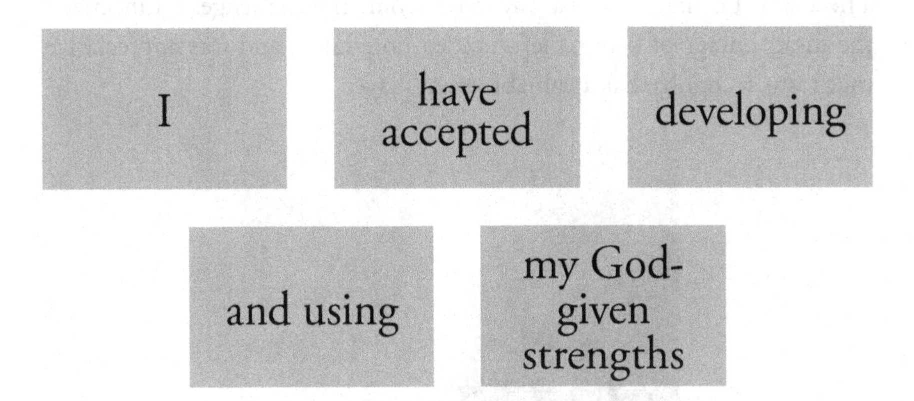

When entering the work world, I was subliminally aware of my left-handedness and challenges and wanted to "just do my best, and let God do the rest." I was able to succeed at job performance and even offered more opportunities and salary advances than I expected.

Even though I was mostly the "wind beneath the wings" of supervisors and co-workers, there were a few times I may have been in the soaring role of an eagle, helping make decisions. More than once in my working career, I was told that I have a special gift in accomplishments in my working career. Two gifts I believe I have identified may not be a derivative from being right-brained, but true gifts from God to allow me to overcome the challenges:

- Learning skills such as shorthand and typing and being able to increase speeds desirable for being hired by employers.
- Being able to perceive and quickly grasp the subject area that was being discussed or studied and quickly seeing the point of the matter along with the art of taking notes, and to quickly transcribe notes after a meeting. The ability to produce minutes and notes grammatically correct which grasped the main points and concluding discussion was appreciated, and I was called on as the "note-taker" by more than one supervisor in my different types of employment during my working years.

The following picture illustrates the challenge of taking notes with the left-hand when using the spiral bound shorthand notebook! Where there was a necessity, I usually found a way to overcome the challenge. I minimized the disadvantage of being a left-handed note-taker, and was appreciative that I was recognized as a valuable team player.

Writing challenge of left hander

One training seminar for notary public staff had a comment made by the trainer, that in past centuries, the person with the most power in the room was the note-taker! I had always tried to be diligent and do my best at this task.

Another supervisor who once nominated me for employee of the quarter, told me after I was chosen by the nomination committee, that he thought it was long overdue that I should have that designation.

And another supervisor said that sometimes she would wonder if I was getting everything down, but the notes documented that I "never missed a beat" in the recording of the meeting. Another supervisor said he really appreciated that I was on the quiet side, which is very valuable in the role of a confidential secretary. There were some business occurrences and events that heavily depended on confidentiality except through the appropriate designated spokesperson. Can you believe it – my quietness was an asset to the employer!!

Once when I left an employer to begin a new job, a co-worker gave me the following note, which meant a lot to me:

"You will be missed so much. I can't tell you how much it has meant to have you helping out at the front desk. Your Godly attitude has shown through in many ways. I know you'll be appreciated wherever you go. I know you are a great loss to the department and your friends here."

Other accomplishments include being elected secretary of the classified school employees association, as well as being a secretary for the educational foundation. This position was a community outreach and was very important in being a good liaison between the school budget needs and the contributions from the community.

My point is not to boast, but to point out that I, like many other left-handers in this right-handed world have adapted and used the God-given gifts that are beneficial, valued, and appreciated. Some things I cannot do well, but some things I can do very well.

Recently I came across information on the internet about Business Etiquette, and some of the right brain/left brain characteristics were presented. It is considerate among co-workers to allow for difference of perspective and ideas!

Whatever the Brain Dominance - TAKE CARE OF YOUR HEALTH: Drink Water, Eat Beneficial Foods and Exercise!

As the Bible tells us… love God, love others as yourself. I believe this includes loving yourself enough to appreciate learning about healthy habits to stay healthy. (And as my friend always reminds me—drink water!)

There are many sources of information and self-help education I have come across. Here is one that I found particularly interesting:

"The Wild Nightlife of the Brain"

"The brain is made up of nervous tissue that relies on the glucose supplies produced by the rest of the body to function. As the command center for the entire body, it can be argued that the rest of the body processes energy primarily to fuel the brain."

Further learning from the book entitled Anticancer Living, Transform Your Life and Health with the Mix of Six, by Lorenzo Cohen, PhD, and Alison Jefferies, documents their science research which uncovered the importance of healthy habits; and one of the Mix of Six involves the brain and the importance of an adequate amount of sleep.

As documented in the book, there is an activity that intensifies in the brain during a person's SLEEP: the natural essential brain cleansing of toxins and waste which accumulate during waking hours.

It dawned on me that no matter the dominance of the computerized-like energy flow in brain "wiring" – left brain/right hand, or right brain/left hand, or ambidextrous (as someone recently stated to me that he could use power tools such as saws, hammers, nail guns used in his construction job with either hand), it seems that when a person's best "power tools" are needed, whether mental, physical, or both, the right amount of sleep is important.

Note to ponder: perhaps this period of brain rest is when solutions to problems come to us – often in the middle of the night – as the brain cleanses itself and clarity comes.

Acknowledge and Accept the Difference

Possibly some lefties, like me, have often or subliminally felt "less-than" or somehow not good enough to do some things due to having a left hand disadvantage.

My advice to a leftie is: acknowledge and accept the difference. Left-handedness is not a disability or a condition. It is just different. There are some things a left hander may never be as good at doing, and possibly some right handers who also feel unable to excel at an aspiration.

If you become aware that you could use some assistance, ask for and accept the help from someone or from God's intervening hand (through family, church family, professionals, or others).

Accept the difference and accept the help if needed and offered.

Conversely, help someone else if it is needed and requested.

PART THREE

PERHAPS THE "PERSPECTIVE OF GOD"

CHAPTER 5

God the Creator and His Creations – God created EVERYTHING…

<u>Including</u> Right and Left Brain individuals

You are likely a believer in God or at least in an Intelligent Design or you would not have read this far!

The creation is recorded in the Bible in Genesis 1-2:3:

And God saw that it was good.

So the man gave names to all the livestock, the birds of the air and all the beasts of the field.

Other Interesting Creation Facts

On the subject of the Creator and His creation/creatures, it is interesting that there are many creatures that have abilities or functions that logically could not have "evolved" from the evolution theory. Many animals and insects have self-protection abilities and are truly amazing and noteworthy of study. I believe some scientists ultimately come to the realization that intelligent design must be responsible for creation and not happenstance of the evolution theory. This controversial topic can be further researched if you desire to do so.

Miracles set in Place!

God's creations during the first six days included formation of the ecosystem miracles set in place; including the last one of the creation in God's image – man and woman! The innate abilities - mental, physical, spiritual - are truly astonishing and amazing and everything is in harmonious works together. According to the Bible, there is not a single thing or creature in existence that God did not intentionally create.

The more we learn about history and current scientific and faith-acceptance knowledge, the more we should naturally worship and praise the Creator for His creations.

Helixes and Spirals throughout Nature and the Universe

Other fascinating creations are helixes and spirals throughout the universe and nature (for example climbing plants, some rock formations, and seashells.) I have read that most climbing plants spiral to the right, but the Honeysuckle spirals to the left; and I recently learned that some sunflowers have a double helix spiral. If God created the right- and left- helix spirals throughout nature, why not create the potential of right-handed and left-handed people? An observation of interest is that most people have a cowlick (maybe more than one) with their head of hair that spirals to the right or to the left. I have heard that cowlicks that spiral to the left are relevant to left-handedness. It is documented that left-hand helixes and spirals are far less common throughout nature, just as left-handed people are far less common in nature. Maybe there is a proportionate correlation and reason. Reference is made to the Addendum Notes for more information.

Is DNA God's Knitting?

The DNA structured like fabric in a ribbon band – reminds me of fabric Tapestry.

Another relatively new area of research is DNA. If you look for information on "Z-DNA", there are some very interesting structures. There is A-DNA,

B-DNA, and left-handed Z-DNA. When observing the composition of the different DNA models, it seems the A-DNA and B-DNA relative composition are double strands and comparable to "tapestry." However, the Z-DNA seems to have "zig-zag", making it seem to have an incompletely formed width. I would like to think the DNA strands hold the personality traits, talents, abilities, soul and spirit which were knitted together in the womb, and in the image of God. When looking at the DNA spiraled strands from the side, the comparisons are very interesting. When looking at the DNA from the top down view, they are all fascinating, with the Z-DNA seeming to be so much more complex and beautifully arranged.

Take a moment to search and look at DNA on the internet!

Left-Handers mentioned in the Bible

There are a couple of different views regarding the mention of left-handed people in the Bible, whose words and deeds impacted the status quo and possibly the governing state of affairs. So, I personally believe that God knows the difference between left and right-handedness. The Bible refers to left-handed on several occasions, including: the story of 700 Benjaminites who could use the sling with deadly accuracy, the story of Ehud and also the story of two-dozen ambidextrous warriors who came to support David in Hebron (1 Chronicles 12:2).

700 Left-Handed Men

One of the recorded incidents is in Judges 20. There were 700 left-handed men, hand picked due to their skill level.

Ehud, A Left-Handed Man

It may be that the Bible story illustrates God's resourceful means to accomplish a goal as recorded in Judges 3:15. The Israelites were at times pleasing and worshipping God, then falling away and worshiping idols, being punished, and needing to be "rescued" out of the hands of evil power. God used a unique person, Ehud, a left-handed man, who was the second Judge in Israel. He made his way through the security of a cruel

King who had become oppressive over the last 18 years of ruling over Israel. Perhaps because he was left-handed he was advantaged by hiding his weapon on his right side, making his way through the routine, normal security system surrounding the King. Ehud gained access to the King by stating that he had a tribute for the king. When the king had allowed Ehud audience, Ehud caught the King off guard, and killed him with his sword. This freed the Israelites from the oppressive, evil King's control and led to peace for Israel, which lasted 80 years.

Some may conclude these two Old Testament recordings illustrate the sinister nature of the left-handed. However, I choose to conclude that God disperses left-handed creations throughout the world, and then at times chooses the appropriate person(s) to accomplish His purpose.

God summarizes His creations and reminds his servant Job:

Creator's authority and power – God's Animals have Instincts, Personality and Character Traits

The Lord answered Job out of the storm. He reminded Job that he doesn't know everything – he doesn't know what he does not know. In fact, Job soon realized from God's lesson that there is a lot he did not know. It seems that God brought to Job's attention almost every animal, great and small, that has been created. God skillfully and artfully had put in the instincts and characteristics (See Addendum Notes - Job – chapters 38 through 41)

Visit a Zoo or a wildlife preserve!

The next time you visit a zoo or observe in nature God's creations, from safari-type animals to domesticated animals, you may want to spend a little time reflecting on the differences and similarities. What can be learned from God's creations? There are some beautiful and amazing creatures! As a friend commented, it would be interesting to observe monkeys, apes, etc. to see which hand they use when picking up things.

PART FOUR

CONCLUDING THOUGHTS– AUTHOR'S PERSPECTIVE AGAIN

CHAPTER 6

Appreciate – Be Thankful!

Left-handers "Scattered" throughout Society?

So, how many lefties are there now, in the United States and other countries of the world?

The criterion seems to be which hand is used for writing, as the chief measuring standard to rely on for classifying as a lefty. However, we will never know how many people were born to be lefties, but learned how to write with their right hand.

Why or if left-handers are scattered throughout society, it may just be that God wanted it that way! Perhaps in past history appearing sinister, clumsy, awkward creations – they are only left-handers living in a mostly right-handed world. More research always reveals interesting knowledge to meditate on.

If you know a left-hander I hope you realize that they may be special game-changers to be appreciated for their different way of viewing the world. Acknowledge and accept their differences.

The hand, of course, does not determine anything by itself. I think basically innate handedness goes back to the dominant brain hemisphere, which goes back to DNA, which goes back to God the Creator.

I think our bodies and our brains are amazingly complex, but God knows His designs. No matter what form of communication (hearing, touch, smell, invention of written languages), it is still a mystery to me regarding how our brain hemispheres perceive and receive and then interpret information. Maybe the right-brain "creative factor" begins when information or communication awareness first makes illuminating or activation contact in some degree with the right-brain hemisphere, before being influenced by the intellect of the left-brain hemisphere. And, maybe the reverse is true when the information or communication awareness first makes illuminating or activation contact in some degree with the left-brain hemisphere, before being influenced by the intellect of the right-brain hemisphere.

Concluding Thoughts: Appreciate Current Research

Be thankful there is enlightened acceptance of left-handedness. There is hope on the horizon! Maybe due to current research, more individuals who are left-handed do not feel so "branded", and the ratios of left-handed and right-handed are becoming more equal.

I recently met a new, beginning, elementary school teacher who is from another country. I was asking her about left-handedness in her country, and she said there are no left-handed – she was not familiar with left-handedness. However, she said she noticed some of her students she said "writing funny" and asked if that was why, because they are left-handed. She handed me her contact information and said she is interested in learning about left-handedness and asked if I would include something in this book that will help teachers.

This brings up the cultural view on handedness – I am not sure what multi-cultural studies have been done on handedness and what it means in different countries. Sounds like this could be another book topic!

I have in the past several years made acquaintances with individuals from different countries and have discussed handedness. It seems in some cultures, early identification of left-handed writing necessitates re-directing or training of that learner to use the right hand for writing. I also find it interesting that different cultures' learners may write in a row from the left side of the page across to the right side. Then again, some cultures' learners write from the right side of the page to the left side of the page. A friend commented to me that beginning in the 1950's the handwriting of her language changed from beginning at the top of the page ending at the bottom of the page in a column; now learners are taught to write across in a row, from the left side of the page ending at the right of the page.

I am thankful that there is knowledge and progress being made in the educational field relating to the communication between the two brains, right and left, between the more dominant hemisphere and the less dominant hemisphere and the natural differences in right and left handers. Diagnosis, counseling, and therapy/training are within reach. I believe there is a correlation between the right-brain, left-brain, and types of learning and teaching strategies and that our body's energy benefits from kinesiology movement.

Again, the previously mentioned videos that I came across on the internet and YouTube information (and I agree with) of academic research regarding the dyslexic brain are providing for insight for educational training and careers:

'How a Dyslectic Brain Works – A Simple Demonstration' by KinaLearn on YouTube.com and

'The True Gifts of a Dyslexic Mind' by Dean Bragonier, TEDxMarthasVineyard also on YouTube.com

Another website, www.dyslexia.com has a very informative article about The Dyslexic Brain – Wired for Whole Brain Thinking.

"Scientists can now capture images of the internal wiring of the brain, using a tool called 'diffusion tensor imaging' (DTI). Research can now confirm what was once only a hypothesis: the dyslexic brain is wired differently, in a way that is far more elegant than a mere localized glitch or disruption." And again, I personally think left-handed individuals do have a higher possibility of dyslexia."

Accentuate the positive strengths and weaknesses. Research and ask for help if needed to accomplish goals.

As stated earlier, in the past five to seven decades, left-handers have come to be more understood, valued and appreciated and this may be likely largely due to many sports figures and television to be able to see them perform on a mass level like never before in history.

My conclusion

Be mindful and thankful for differences in design with purpose in God's creations. Go, put a smile on your face each day. Go, put a smile on God's face – show him how thankful you are for all he has made and done for us, the signs and wonders, and created in his image! Picture him in his majestic garment with His train across heaven, looking at us.

Even the energy in all creation nature declares the glory of God, Psalm 96. I believe everything is composed of energy, and even one young observer I know has noticed a "hum" of the energy in stars, and the whispering of the wind energy blowing through the tree tops!

Read John 3:16 which tells us the reason God is helping us on earth. Read Acts Chapter 1 and Chapter 2, which tells how to be added to Jesus Christ's church family. Search for the principles and morsels of treasures by learning about God. Find a Bible-based church group to become part of, and thank God for creating church family where we can escape from the daily grind and enjoy the blessing of group meet (the assembly of the first born.) Hebrews 12:23

Volunteer to give a helping hand to a cause you believe in. There are many organizations and activities that request help. Sometimes there is even instruction or training to help volunteers be more effective and valuable.

Remember, the only thing we leave this world with is our knowledge, wisdom... We brought nothing into the world, and will leave with nothing, only what we became in life. We may not be able to change the past, but knowledge and free-will choices we make today can change the future.

Every "tick-tock" of the clock reminds me of the importance of now. Remember there is no reset or do-over when we leave this earth life; surround yourself and look for the positive things while in this life.

The Bible includes Instructions for Life

Read Proverbs 3:16 regarding the value of wisdom and understanding: "Long life is in her right hand, in her left hand are riches and honor."

Right handers who became left handers due to some life-altering event: Go, make us proud by going about daily tasks and obligations, by your contributing to the left-hand minority.

Appreciate that there are left-handers (possible dyslectic brain individuals) who are mingled throughout society which adds spice to life: game changers for bad or good. Individuals uniquely vary from person to person.

We are all God's children and are going through life's journey together!

Be a seeker - renew your spirit each day, as God renews the earth's landscape each day. Every day is different as affirmed by looking up at the ever-changing skyscape and enjoying the changing landscape by looking around at nature! Let the Holy Spirit help you keep the two new commandments given in Matthew 22:37-40:

1. Love God;
2. Love people.

SUCCESS

"To laugh often and much; to win the respect of intelligent people and the affection of children; to earn the appreciation of honest critics and endure the betrayal of false friends; to appreciate beauty, to find the best in others; to leave the world a bit better, whether by a healthy child, a garden patch or a redeemed social condition; to know even one life has breathed easier because you have lived. This is to have succeeded."

--poem by Ralph Waldo Emerson

With God's help through Jesus Christ my savior, and the guidance and comfort of the Holy Spirit…, I have succeeded! Without knowledge, we perish: Hosea 4:6

Some of my favorite Bible verses:

Genesis 1:1
John 3:16-21
John 14:27
Malachi
Matthew 5:1-12 and Matthew 7:7-8
Acts 2:1-42
Philippians 4:4-9
Hebrews 13:20-21
James 1
Revelation 22

PART FIVE

ADDENDUM NOTES, AND RESEARCH AND SOURCE INFORMATION

I have tried various ways to contact the copyright holder for permission to use this material; all is attributable to the author(s) who published the book(s) for our enlightenment and information.

Addendum Section A
Article "Life on the Left"

Here is an excerpt from the book, Writing: Craft and Art, obviously written by a lefty. I would really be interested in meeting the writer!

"Ever since I was a baby, kicking and gurgling at the world from my crib, my parents knew I was left-handed…they'd offer me my bottle, or a toy, or just a finger to play with, … I got more food in my mouth left-handed, I banged more loudly on the left side of my crib…So it was that I earned my membership in a select group of people…. Members of my organization are not hard to pick out in a crowd – we're the ones who sit at the far end of dinner tables, the ones who write with pen and paper at all sorts of different angles, the ones who tell time by the wrong wrist…."

The "right" way is what about nine out of ten people do, although doctors and psychologists are still puzzled over the reason for such a large right-handed majority. Presently, it is believed that one out of three children is born with a tendency toward left-handedness, but that parents coax their children to adjust to the right- handed world, and so cut down the troops in the left-handed army.

Interestingly enough, the tendency of a society toward predominant right-handedness seems to be universal: the ancient Greeks and Romans, Eskimos, Africans, Indians – all are right-handed. It seems that the language-makers of these and other societies remind left-handers they are outnumbered. Our word "right" suggests some inherent correctness in using the right hand, while the left hand is "left out" of most tasks. The French word for right, *droit*, also means just, or honest, and is the root for our word "adroit," while their word for left, *gauche*, means awkward. In German, *link* for left also means awkward, and *recht* for right is like the English "right" – just and true.

… Each day a left-hander receives a barrage of reminders that the rest of the world is doing things differently…."

Addendum Section B
Helixes, Spirals, Cowlicks (tufts of hair that are not easily manageable!)

The following is from The Left-Handers' Handbook by James Bliss and Joseph Morella.

"People, as we know, have strong preferences for [handedness]. P. 49

"Hand" preference in nature – since rocks, plants and animals do not possess hands – expresses itself most basically in terms of the helix, a spiral curve through a cylindrical or conical shape. The helix may turn to the right, in a clockwise direction, or to the left, counter-clockwise.P. 49

Amino acids, for example, the essential components of proteins, are invariable left-spiraled in living tissue. In short, life on this planet has been structured with the left preference as an integral part of the master plan. P. 49

Another example is that table sugar (dextrose) is right-spiraled. Fructose, occurring in honey and many fruits, is different from dextrose only in that it spirals to the left. P 49

Plant stems and stalks, even leaves, flowers and stems, may be formed in the pattern of these three-dimensional curves. Leaves may be attached to the stalk in a spiral that is a clockwise or counter-clockwise helix. P 50

In climbing plants such as vines, the helix pattern is impossible to overlook. The twining and trailing plants of the genus Convolvulus were even named for their convolutions or coils. Members of this genus (bindweed and morning-glory) attempt to climb in a right-handed fashion, and most twisting plants stick to a consistent system of climbing and coiling in the same direction as other members of their species. Honeysuckle, for example, appears to be consistently left-helixed. The spectacle of left-handed honey-suckle crisscrossing with right-handed bindweed, as they climb a common support, has inspired… poetic comment as long as four centuries ago, when the English dramatist Ben Jonson observed: "The blue bindweed doth itself enfold with honeysuckle. P. 51

Left-handed and right-handed spirals can be seen on the bark of beech trees and chestnuts, as well as on the trunks of many evergreens. These helixes seem to go either way, clockwise or counterclockwise, for no apparent reason. As we said before, Nature is not biased. P. 51

Helixes can be seen in …the beautiful coiled shells of mollusks such as snails. The coils may twist to the left or to the right. Even extinct mollusk …discovered by geologists, had shells with helixes turning in both directions. As in the plant world, members of one species usually all make their patterns in the same direction. But strange variations may happen. Occasionally a species will be left-handed in one part of the world, right-oriented in another geographic location….p 51

What can we conclude from all this? Left-right preferences do exist in the natural world, in inanimate matter, plants and animals....P. 57

I recently learned that some sunflowers have a double helix. Close inspection reveals a helix of one direction, and also a helix going in the other direction.

On a sidenote, contemplating writing this book, I was at my hairdresser appointment and thought of dyeing my hair gray – perhaps it would give me more wisdom! My hairdresser said she could probably count the grey hair I have. And, she verified that my "cowlick" in my hair does swirl to the left.

Addendum Section C
Handedness information

TESTS for HANDEDNESS, some excerpts from "<u>The Left-Handers' Handbook</u>

<u>ACTIVITIES</u>

#1. Hands:

Quickly clasp your hands together, interlocking fingers. Do it without looking. Now look down as your hands. Which thumb is on top?

#2 Hands:

Get a pencil and a sheet of paper. Now draw two circles – one with your right hand, one with your left. Now look at the direction in which you drew the circles: clockwise? Counterclockwise? One of each?

<u>ANSWERS</u>

#1: Hands

Is the hand with the uppermost thumb your left hand? If so, chances are that you are a lefty—even if you write with your right hand.

#2: Hands

If with either hand you drew a clockwise circle, you have some tendencies toward left-handedness. Most people who are completely right-handed will draw both circles counterclockwise.

Addendum Section D
Research Information from Wikipedia regarding Methods of thinking (Critical thinking and Spatial Lateral Thinking – Author's note: This is interesting information, but even though I do not understand all of it!)

<u>Critical thinking</u> is primarily concerned with judging the truth value of statements and seeking errors. Lateral thinking is more concerned with the "movement value" of statements and ideas. A person uses lateral thinking to move from one known idea to creating new ideas. Edward de Bono defines four types of thinking tools:

1. idea-generating tools intended to break current thinking patterns—routine patterns, the status quo
2. focus tools intended to broaden where to search for new ideas
3. harvest tools intended to ensure more value is received from idea generating output
4. treatment tools that promote consideration of real-world constraints, resources, and support[]

Random Entry Idea Generating Tool

The thinker chooses an object at random, or a noun from a dictionary, and associates it with the area they are thinking about. De Bono gives the example the randomly-chosen word "nose" being applied to an office photocopier, leading to the idea that the copier could produce a lavender smell when it was low on paper, to alert staff.[4]

Provocation Idea Generating Tool

A provocation is a statement that we know is wrong or impossible but use to create new ideas. De Bono gives an example of considering river pollution and setting up the provocation "the factory is downstream of itself"; this leads to the idea of forcing a factory to take its water input from a point downstream of its output, an idea which later became law in some countries.[5] Provocations can be set up by the use of any of the provocation techniques—wishful thinking, exaggeration, reversal, escape, distortion, or arising. The thinker creates a list of provocations and then uses the most outlandish ones to move their thinking forward to new ideas.

Movement Techniques

One can move from a provocation to a new idea by the following methods: extract a principle, focus on the difference, moment to moment, positive aspects, special circumstances.

Challenge Idea Generating Tool

A tool which is designed to ask the question "Why?" in a non-threatening way: why something exists, why it is done the way it is. The result is a very clear understanding of "Why?" which naturally leads to fresh new ideas. The goal is to be able to challenge anything at all, not just items which are problems. For example, one could challenge the handles on coffee cups: The reason for the handle seems to be that the cup is often too hot to hold directly; perhaps coffee cups could be made with insulated finger grips, or there could be separate coffee-cup holders similar to beer holders, or coffee shouldn't be so hot in the first place.

Concept From Idea Generating Tool

Ideas carry out concepts. This tool systematically expands the range and number of concepts in order to end up with a very broad range of ideas to consider.

Disproving

Based on the idea that the majority is always wrong (as suggested by Henrik Ibsen[6] and by John Kenneth Galbraith[7]), take anything that is obvious and generally accepted as "goes without saying", question it, take an opposite view, and try to convincingly disprove it. This technique is similar to de Bono's "Black Hat" of *Six Thinking Hats*, which looks at identifying reasons to be cautious and conservative.

Addendum Section E
Problem solving

Problem Solving

When something creates a problem, the performance or the status quo of the situation drops. Problem solving deals with finding out what caused the problem and then figuring out ways to fix the problem. The objective is to get the situation to where it should be. For example, a production line has an established run rate of 1000 items per hour. Suddenly, the run rate drops to 800 items per hour. Ideas as to why this happened and solutions to repair the production line must be thought of, such as giving the worker a pay raise.

Creative Problem Solving

Using creativity, one must solve a problem in an indirect and unconventional manner. For example, if a production line produced 1000 books per hour, creative problem solving could find ways to produce more books per hour, use the production line, or reduce the cost to run the production line.

Creative Problem Identification

Many of the greatest non-technological innovations are identified while realizing an improved process or design in everyday objects and tasks either by accidental chance or by studying and documenting real world experience.

Lateral Problem "Solving"

Lateral thinking will often produce solutions whereby the problem appears as "obvious" in hindsight. That lateral thinking will often lead to problems that you never knew you had, or it will solve simple problems that have a huge potential. For example, if a production line produced 1000 books per hour, lateral thinking may suggest that a drop in output to 800 would lead to higher quality, more motivated workers etc. etc.

Lateral thinking puzzles

These are puzzles that are supposed to demonstrate what lateral thinking is about. However any puzzle that has only one solution is "not" lateral. While lateral thinking may help you construct such puzzles, the lateral thinking tools will seldom help you solve puzzles.

See also Wikipedia 5/1/17

Addedum Section F
Kinesiology and movement based energy balance. Much information can be learned through surfing the internet.

Interesting information is available about cross patterning and movement based activities for all ages. Do some research on the internet.

Addendum Section G
Life Skills Program

A life skills program provides opportunity for individuals to learn a great number of psychosocial skills. These skills will give the capability to meet the demands of modern adulthood.

What kind of Essential Life Skills?

Decision Making
Problem Solving
Creative Thinking
Critical Thinking
Effective Communication
Interpersonal Relationships
Self Awareness and Mindfulness
Assertiveness
Empathy for and Helping Others
Equanimity
Coping with Stress, Trauma and Loss
Resilience

Lifestyle includes personal hygiene, cooking meals, cleaning a kitchen, and washing clothes. It also, includes car upkeep, finding a place to live, and food shopping.

Communication will teach basic manners, dating and relationships, interpersonal communications, workplace communication.

Personal Development covers stress management, anger management, self-esteem, conflict resolution, the importance of family, and the impacts of lying and disrespect.

Nutrition will help teach proper diet and food handling.

Money Management focuses on managing money, filing taxes, borrowing money, credit, financial assistance for education, and checking and savings accounts.

Addendum Section H
Special for Left-Handers

There are products for lefties that can be obtained from stores featuring left-handed products. Using some left-handed bias items may provide some skill and comfort (i.e. left-hand scissors allow for seeing the cutting line).

Information is available on the internet. See also International Left Handers Day recognized on August 13 each year.

Addendum Section I
Nibs.com: Fountain Pens and Left-HandedWriters

For the full articles, look at the website information section

PENnant Article - Left-Hand Writers

This is an excerpt from an article submitted to The PENnant, the magazine of Pen Collectors of America for the winter 2000 issue.

Notes from the Nib Works
Left-handed Writers
revised 6/8/04

Faced with more obstacles, left-handers become adapters. This is certainly true of their writing. Cursive western writing is performed from left to right and, because they tend to dig into the paper more when they are pushed, fountain pens are harder to push than to pull. Left-handers must push their fountain pens at least some of the time, while a right-handed person pulls or draws most of their marks. Add to this trouble the problem of slow drying ink, and left-handed people are sometimes faced with ink stained palms as well.

left-handers…develop numerous strategies to compensate. Some turn their left hand hard to the right, so that they write over top of the line…overwriters turn their paper so that they write away from themselves, …another…strategy southpaws hold the pen below the line…. These "underwriters" have several variants. If the paper is placed squarely in front, most underwriters must push their pens into the paper. If the top of the paper is turned radically to the right, to give more comfort to the hand and a better direction for the point, the writing is seen as coming down toward the writer at a sharp angle....

Because of the variety of unique approaches lefties bring to their writing, (and to their lives, for that matter) any generalizations made about left-hand people are sure to be wrong for more than a few individuals. Left-handed people run against the grain of our physical world. For this reason they frequently think differently….handle our world in unconventional ways….

The right and left hemisphere studies of the brain relate the left side of our bodies to the right brain. Intuitive thought and spatial relations are believed to reside there. The physical process of writing is handled in the area of spatial attention, giving left-handed writers a more direct mode for writing. …other brain studies suggest that a greater number of left-handed people have more cross over between the hemispheres of the brain. This is where, many researchers believe, much creative thought is generated, especially the kind of thought used by artists and architects…."

An excerpt from another article from the Nibs.Com information states that …when you're writing from left to right, such as with the English language, left-handed writers need to avoid dragging their hand through the drying ink. Lefties are clever and tend to avoid this instinctively. It doesn't even cross their mind that they've developed a strategy to get along in a predominantly right-handed world."

Addendum Section J

There are different Bible translations which may vary a little in the translation; this Addendum Section is from the New International Version.

In the Beginning…

The creation of the ecosystems are recorded in the Bible.

Genesis 1

In the beginning God created the heavens and the earth. Now the earth was formless and empty, darkness was over the surface of the deep, and the Spirit of God was hovering over the waters.

And God said, "Let there be light," and there was light. God saw that the light was good, and he separated the light from the darkness. God called the light "day," and the darkness he called "night." And there was evening, and there was morning - the first day.

And God said, "let there be an expanse between the waters to separate water from water." So God made the expanse and separated the water under the expanse from the water above it. And it was so. God called the expanse "sky." And there was evening, and there was morning - the second day.

And God said, "Let the water under the sky be gathered to one place, and let dry ground appear." And it was so. God called the dry ground "land," and the gathered waters he called "seas." And God saw that it was good. Then God said, "Let the land produce vegetation: seed-bearing plants and trees on the land that bear fruit with seed in it, according to their various kinds." And it was so. The land produced vegetation: plants bearing seed according to their kinds and trees bearing fruit with seed in it according to their kinds. And God saw that it was good. And there was evening, and there was morning - the third day.

And God said, "Let there be lights in the expanse of the sky to separate the day from the night, and let them serve as signs to mark seasons and days and years, and let them be lights in the expanse of the sky to give light on the earth." And it was so. God made two great lights – the greater light to govern the day and the lesser light to govern the night. He also made the stars. God set them in the expanse of the sky to give light on the earth, to govern the day and the night, and to separate light from darkness. And God saw that it was good. And there was evening, and there was morning – the fourth day.

And God said, "Let the water teem with living creatures, and let birds fly above the earth across the expanse of the sky." So God created the great creatures of the sea and every living and moving thing with which the water teems, according to their kinds, and every winged bird according to its kind. And God saw that it was good.

God blessed them and said, "Be fruitful and increase in number and fill the water in the seas, and let the birds increase on the earth." And there was evening, and there was morning – the fifth day.

And God said, "Let the land produce living creatures according to their kinds: livestock, creatures that move along the ground, and wild animals, each according to its kind." And it was so. God made the wild animals according to their kinds, the livestock according to their kinds, and all the creatures that move along the ground according to their kinds. And God saw that it was good.

Then God said, "Let us make man in our image, in our likeness, and let them rule over the fish of the sea and the birds of the air, over the livestock, over all the earth, and over all the creatures that move along the ground."

So God created man in his own image, in the image of God he created him: male and female he created them.

God blessed them and said to them, "Be fruitful and increase in number; fill the earth and subdue it. Rule over the fish of the sea and the birds of the air and over every living creature that moves on the ground."

Then God said, "I give you every seed-bearing plant on the face of the whole earth and every tree that has fruit with seed in it. They will be yours for food. And to all the beasts of the earth and all the birds of the air and all the creatures that move on the ground – everything that has the breath of life in it – I give every green plant for food." And it was so.

God saw all that he had made, and it was very good. And there was evening, and there was morning – the sixth day.

Genesis Chapter 2:

1. Thus the heavens and the earth were completed in all their vast array.
2. By the seventh day God had finished the work he had been doing; so on the seventh day he rested from all his work.
3. And God blessed the seventh day and made it holy, because on it he rested from all the work of creating that he had done.
4. This is the account of the heavens and the earth when they were created. When the Lord God made the earth and the heavens--
5. And no shrub of the field had yet appeared on the earth and no plant of the field had yet sprung up, for the Lord God had not sent rain on the earth and there was no man to work the ground,
6. But streams came up from the earth and watered the whole surface of the ground—
7. The Lord God formed the man from the dust of the ground and breathed into his nostrils the breath of life, and the man became a living being.
8. Now the Lord God had planted a garden in the east, in Eden; and there he put the man he had formed.
9. And the Lord God made all kinds of trees grow out of the ground - - trees that were pleasing to the eye and good for food. In the middle of the garden were the tree of life and the tree of the knowledge of good and evil.
10. A river watering the garden flowed from Eden; from there it was separated into four headwaters.
11. The name of the first is the Pishon; it winds through the entire land of Havilah, where there is gold.

12. (The gold of that land is good; aromatic resin and onyx are also there.)
13. The name of the second river is the Gihon; it winds through the entire land of Cush.
14. The name of the third river is the Tigris; it runs along the east side of Asshur. And the fourth river is the Euphrates.

Creator's authority and power – Questions about Personality and Character Traits

God summarizes his creations and reminds his servant Job:

Job – Chapters 38 through 41

In the book of Job, the Lord answered Job out of the storm. He reminded Job that he doesn't know everything – he doesn't know what he does not know. The Lord said:

"Who is this that darkens my counsel with words without knowledge? Brace yourself like a man; I will question you, and you shall answer me."

God proceeds to ask Job about the creation, the laws of the heavens; who set up God's dominion over the earth, who endowed the heart with wisdom or gave understanding to the mind? Was Job the one who created all or was it the Lord?

Job 38

Then the Lord answered Job out of the storm. He said:

"Who is this that darkens my counsel with words without knowledge?

Brace yourself like a man; I will question you, and you shall answer me."

"Where were you when I laid the earth's foundation?

Tell me, if you understand, Who marked off its dimensions? Surely you know!

Who stretched a measuring line across it?

On what were its footings set, or who laid its cornerstone - -

While the morning stars sang together and all the angels shouted for joy?

“Who shut up the sea behind doors when it burst forth from the womb,

When I made the clouds its garment and wrapped it in thick darkness,

When I fixed limits for it and set its doors and bars in place,

When I said, “This far you may come and no farther; here is where your proud waves halt”?

“Have you ever given orders to the morning, or shown the dawn its place,

That it might take the earth by the edges and shake the wicked out of it?

The earth takes shape like clay under a seal; its features stand out like those of a garment.

The wicked are denied their light, and their upraised arm is broken.

“Have you journeyed to the springs of the sea or walked in the recesses of the deep?

Have the gates of death been shown to you? Have you seen the gates of the shadow of death?

Have you comprehended the vast expanses of the earth? Tell me, if you know all this.

“What is the way to the abode of light? And where does darkness reside? Can you take them to their places? Do you know the paths to their dwellings?

Surely you know, for you were already born! You have lived so many years!

"Have you entered the storehouses of the snow or seen the storehouses of the hail,

Which I reserve for times of trouble, for days of war and battle?

What is the way to the place where the lightning is dispersed, or the place where the east winds are scattered over the earth?

Who cuts a channel for the torrents of rain, and a path for the thunderstorm,

To water a land where no man lives, a desert with no one in it, to satisfy a desolate wasteland

And make it sprout with grass? Does the rain have a father? Who fathers the drops of dew? From whose womb comes the ice? Who gives birth to the frost from the heavens

When the waters become hard as stone, when the surface of the deep is frozen?

"Can you bind the beautiful Pleiades? Can you loose the cords of Orion?

Can you bring forth the constellations in their seasons or lead out the Bear with its cubs?

Do you know the laws of the heavens? Can you set up God's dominion over the earth?

Can you raise your voice to the clouds and cover yourself with a flood of water?

Do you send the lightning bolts on their way? Do they report to you, "Here we are"?

Who endowed the heart with wisdom or gave understanding to the mind?

Who has the wisdom to count the clouds? Who can tip over the water jars of the heavens

When dust becomes hard and the clods of earth stick together?

"Do you hunt the prey for the lioness and satisfy the hunger of the lions when they crouch in their dens

Or lie in wait in a thicket?

Who provides food for the raven when its young cry out to God and wander about for lack of food?"

Job 39

"Do you know when the mountain goats give birth?

Do you watch when the doe bears her fawn?

Do you count the months till they bear?

Do you know the time they give birth?

They crouch down and bring forth their young;

Their labor pains are ended.

Their young thrive and grow strong in the wilds; they leave and do not return.

"Who let the wild donkey go free? Who untied his ropes?

I gave him the wasteland as his home, the salt flats as his habitat.

He laughs at the commotion in the town; he does not hear a driver's shout.

He ranges the hills for his pasture and searches for any green thing.

"Will the wild ox consent to serve you? Will he stay by your manger at night?

Can you hold him to the furrow with a harness? Will he till the valleys behind you?

Will you rely on him for his great strength? Will you leave your heavy work to him?

Can you trust him to bring in your grain and gather it to your threshing floor?

"The wings of the ostrich flap joyfully, but they cannot compare with the

Pinions and father of the stork.

She lays her eggs on the ground and lets them warm in the sand,

Unmindful that a foot may crush them, that some wild animal may trample them.

She treats her young harshly, as if they were not hers;

She cares not that her labor was in vain, for God did not endow her with wisdom

Or give her a share of good sense.

Yet when she spreads her feathers to run, she laughs at horse and rider.

"Do you give the horse his strength or clothe his neck with a flowing mane?

Do you make him leap like a locust, striking terror with his proud snorting?

He paws fiercely, rejoicing in his strength, and charges into the fray.

He laughs at fear, afraid of nothing; he does not shy away from the sword,

The quiver rattles against his side, along with the flashing spear and lance,

In frenzied excitement he eats up the ground; he cannot stand still when the trumpet sounds,

At the blast of the trumpet he shorts, 'Aha!'

He catches the scent of battle from afar, the shout of commanders and the battle cry,

"Does the hawk take flight by your wisdom and spread his wings toward the south?

Does the eagle soar at your command and build his nest on high?

He dwells on a cliff and stays there at night; a rocky crag is his stronghold,

From there he seeks out his food; his eyes detect it from afar.

His young ones feast on blood, and where the slain are, there is he."

The Lord said to Job:

"Will the one who contends with the Almighty correct him?

Let him who accuses God answer him!"

Then Job answered the Lord:

"I am unworthy - - how can I reply to you? I put my hand over my mouth.

I spoke once, but I have no answer - - twice, but I will say no more."

Then the Lord spoke to Job out of the storm:

"Brace yourself like a man; I will question you, and you shall answer me.

"Would you discredit my justice? Would you condemn me to justify yourself?

Do you have an arm like God's and can your voice thunder like his?

Then adorn yourself with glory and splendor, and clothe yourself in honor and majesty.

Unleash the fury of your wrath, look at every proud man and bring him low,

Look at every proud man and humble him, crush the wicked where they stand.

Bury them all in the dust together; shroud their faces in the grave.

Then I myself will admit to you that your own right hand can save you.

"Look at the behemoth, which I made along with you and which feeds on grass like an ox.

What strength he has in his loins, what power in the muscles of his belly!

His tail sways like a cedar; the sinews of his thighs are close-knit.

His bones are tubes of bronze, his limbs like rods of iron.

He ranks first among the works of God, yet his maker can approach him with his sword.

The hills bring him their produce, and all the wild animals play nearby.

Under the lotus plants he lies, hidden among the reeds in the marsh.

The lotuses conceal him in their shadow; the poplars by the stream surround him.

When the river rages, he is not alarmed; he is secure, though the Jordan should surge against his mouth.

Can anyone capture him by the eyes, or trap him and pierce his nose?"

Job 41:

"Can you pull in the leviathan with a fishhook or tie down his tongue with a rope?

Can you put a cord through his nose or pierce his jaw with a hook?

Will he keep begging you for mercy? Will he speak to you with gentle words?

Will he make an agreement with you for you to take him as your slave for life?

Can you make a pet of him like a bird or put him on a leash for your girls?

Will traders barter for him? Will they divide him up among the merchants?

Can you fill his hide with harpoons or his head with fishing spears?

If you lay a hand on him, you will remember the struggle and never do it again!

Any hope of subduing him is false; the mere sight of him is overpowering.

No one is fierce enough to rouse him.

Who then is able to stand against me? Who has a claim against me that I must pay?

Everything under heaven belongs to me.

"I will not fail to speak of his limbs, his strength and his graceful form.

Who can strip off his outer coat? Who would approach him with a bridle?

Who dares open the doors of his mouth, ringed about with his fearsome teeth?

His back has rows of shields tightly sealed together; each is so close to the next that no air can pass between.

They are joined fast to one another; they cling together and cannot be parted.

His snorting throws out flashes of light; his eyes are like the rays of dawn. Firebrands stream from his mouth; sparks of fire shoot out. Smoke pours from his nostrils as from a boiling pot over a fire of reeds.

His breath sets coals ablaze, and flames dart from his mouth.

Strength resides in his neck; dismay goes before him.

The folds of his flesh are tightly joined; they are firm and immovable.

His chest is hard as rock, hard as a lower millstone.

When he rises up, the mighty are terrified; they retreat before his thrashing.

The sword that reaches him has no effect, nor does the spear or the dart or the javelin.

Iron he treats like straw and bronze like rotten wood.

Arrows do not make him flee; slingstones are like chaff to him.

A club seems to him but a piece of straw; he laughs at the rattling of the lance.

His undersides are jagged potsherds, leaving a trail in the mud like a threshing sledge. He makes the depths churn like a boiling caldron and stirs up the sea like a pot of ointment.

Behind him he leaves a glistening wake; one would think the deep had white hair.

Nothing on earth is his equal - - a creature without fear.

He looks down on all that are haughty; he is king over all that are proud."

The next time you visit a zoo or observe in nature God's creations, you may want to spend a little time reflecting on the differences and similarities. And if God created helix spirals throughout nature, it makes sense that he could create left-handed and right-handed people.

God's creations during the first six days included miracles set in place, just think of the miracles of the creation in God's image – man and woman! The innate abilities, mental, physical, spiritual, are truly to be astonishing and amazing to us human-kind. The more we learn about history and current scientific and faith-acceptance knowledge, the more we worship and praise the Creator for His creations. We worship the Creator and appreciate the creations!

Psalm 96

The World is Firmly Established

[1] Sing to the LORD a new song;
    sing to the LORD, all the earth.

[2] Sing to the LORD, praise his name;
    proclaim his salvation day after day.

[3] Declare his glory among the nations,
    his marvelous deeds among all peoples.

[4] For great is the LORD and most worthy of praise;
he is to be feared above all gods.

[5] For all the gods of the nations are idols,
but the LORD made the heavens.

[6] Splendor and majesty are before him;
strength and glory are in his sanctuary.

[7] Ascribe to the LORD, all you families of nations,
ascribe to the LORD glory and strength.

[8] Ascribe to the LORD the glory due his name;
bring an offering and come into his courts.

[9] Worship the LORD in the splendor of his[a] holiness;
tremble before him, all the earth.

[10] Say among the nations, "The LORD reigns."
The world is firmly established, it cannot be moved;
he will judge the peoples with equity.

[11] Let the heavens rejoice, let the earth be glad;
let the sea resound, and all that is in it.

[12] Let the fields be jubilant, and everything in them;
all the trees of the forest will sing for joy.

[13] They then will sing before the LORD, for he comes,
he comes to judge the earth.

He will judge the world in righteousness
and the peoples in his truth.

Psalm 96:9 Or *Lord with the splendor of*

<u>**New International Version**</u> **(NIV)**

Our Father in heaven,
Hallowed be thy name.
Your Kingdom come,
Your Will be done
on earth as it is in heaven.
Give us this day our daily bread.
Forgive us our debts, as we also have forgiven our debtors.
And Lead us not into temptation, but deliver us from the evil one. NIV

For Thine is the Kingdom, and the Power, and the Glory FOREVER.
Amen!

APPENDIX

References, Acknowledgements, and Attributions:

1. Very special person interview - 12/12/16 and 8/24/18
2. Internet – "Z-DNA" DNA may be a mostly right-handed helix, with left-handed Z-DNA. Research via Wikipedia on Z-DNA is another knowledge-related area which sheds light on one's quest for knowledge. (M.D. text mail received 12-12-16)
3. Internet – YouTube video "How a Dyslexic Brain Works – A Simple Demonstration
4. Internet – YouTube video "The True Gifts of a Dyslexic Mind", talk by Dean Bragonier
5. Internet – website www.Dyslexia.com "The Dyslexic Brain – Wired for Whole Brain Thinking"
6. Scripture taken from the HOLY BIBLE, NEW INTERNATIONAL VERSION c NIV c. Copyright C 1973, 1978, 1984 by International Bible Society. Used by permission of s Bible Society. All rights reserved worldwide.
7. "A Left-Handed History of the World," Ed Wright, 2007 by Murdoch Books Pty Ltd. This 2007 edition published by Metro Books, by arrangement with Murdoch Books Pty Ltd. Metro Books, 122 Fifth Ave. NY, NY 10011 ISBN-13:978-0-7607-8704-5, Printed and bound in China*
8. "The Left-Handers' Handbook," James Bliss & Joseph Morella, Edited by Ann Novotny, first published in the United States in 1980 by A & W Publishers. Inc., 95 Madison Avenue, New York, NY by arrangement with Communication Ventures Inc., printed in the United States of America *

9. Internet - Wikipedia – Spatial and Creative thinking
10. Internet - Website about a Life skills program
11. "Writing: Craft and Art" by William L. Rivers, 1975 by Prentice-Hall, Inc, Englewood Cliffs, New Jersey. Printed in the United States of America.*
12. Paul Dennison Kinesiology website
13. Cohen, Lorenzo PhD and Alison Jefferies, 2018, Anticancer Living, Transform Your Life and Health with the Mix of Six, Viking, an imprint of Penguin Random House LLC, 175-176.
14. L. Xie, H. Kang, Q. Xu, et al., "Sleep drives metabolite clearance from the adult brain," Science 342, no. 6156 (October 2013).
15. NIBS.com website, PENnant article "Left-Handed Writers", 12/18/18
16. Michael Davis, M.S. and PhD student who is a left-handed "achiever" and one of the most thorough detail subject researchers, very knowledgeable about left-hander challenges. His review and insight validates this book's purpose of "encouragement" for left-handers and "enlightenment" for right-handers, and that we are part of the Creator's design
17. Bill and Mary Wilson, right handers who gave feedback to the contents of this book
18. Edith Barnes, retired elementary school teacher, 98 years of experience and wisdom
19. Geri Lou Ronning – Health and Nutrition Consultant
20. Mary Wilcox – review and agreement with the book information
21. Aline Wilson – critiqued by piano player and distinguished musician - English Bells and Tintinnabulation
22. Dow Ferguson, luthier, The Lutherie, and musician playing Guitar, Drum, and Timpani Kettle Drums
23. Summer Nettles – cover artwork
24. Zachary Nettles – photo of right-hander who helps left-handers
25. Review and input from family and friends who either thought this was a good idea or not – to accumulate information for encouragement and enlightenment about left handers.

# # #

*Unable to locate publishers – no information located/closed by proclamation/annulment. Excerpts are in quotations.

Author and right-handed helper!

…got encouragement?: pass it on…
…got knowledge?: pass it on…
# # #

Printed in the United States
By Bookmasters